Sky House

(A transcendental safe space)

Mary Catherine Crouch

Dedication

Thank you to my sweet brother; Chris Jones
For allowing me to stay in your home, which was the inspiration for
the creation of this book

Thankyou to my partner; Mitchell Langdon
For evoking the light within me

Preface

Your whole life
Every choice you ever made
Led you to this moment, right now
Your curious eyes sifting pages
You holding this book
Looking to find some meaning

So I say to you now, dearest reader
If you still believe in coincidence
Put me back
Give me to a friend or throw me in nearest open flames
It makes no difference

For I am not here to convince you
Of any which way of being
Only to extend a potential means of innermost connection
One that cuts through all time, reasoning, fear
A safe space
What you do with your time here, is entirely up to you

Things may get a little darker at times, Just know that the light
is always louder

"There are only two mistakes one can make on the road to truth:
not going all the way,
and not starting."
- Buddha

.emoH emocleW

Chapter 1- The Moss Cottage

Sunlight Prism Compartment- Saturday July 17th 7:08pm

There are ways through this madness
There is a way out
There is a place that you fit

And if right now, you feel like you do not fit anywhere, then let that be
what resonates

This place is of those who have no place
And that place is among many

It is safe

It is meant to be shared
Your life is sacred to earth and to all
Let your breath be a song

A song of light guiding all others home
Home to ourselves
To the small moments of joy shared

Please,
Share who you are

Tuesday July 13th 8:25PM

True love smells like cologne made of warm earth, sunlight, pine
needles & cool laundry breeze
I will keep staring into sunlight
It feels like home it feels like home it feels
like home I am trying to do the right thing
I will become Venus, Goddess of love and
Beauty

May all beings benefit from my light

Eye eye eye

Landscapes and bodies and sculptures
Rich justifications at deeply tormented sounds
The price of gentle awareness
Free and expansive; the islands in which in which we hold ourselves
accountable

To be human
Vulnerable delight of me; indulge
Expand my heart mind so I may be of good use which says nothing
unless it speaks of itself
A gentle volume
I
am wanting
To be as a mother
Loving and kind
Helpful in the right places
Holy mother
Tender of sorrows
Guide my heart
Take mercy on hands
They have far too much to let go of
A sorrow
The journeyful smiles

Passing,
passing

A vast wilderness
I

with my heart mind ripped clean open

Am new to Gods light

I am not an evangelical telemarketer
I do not want your tithe
Just know that beyond all reason
There is goodness outside us
Within us
Is us

It sings happy-bodied landscape hands kept safe in holding,
Every next nothing to lose

Every beautiful thing exists in your eyes

10:10

- Fireflies
- campfires
- Voicemail From People I love
- Sunrises
- The perfect coffee temp
- Long Hugs
- New Art Supplies
- Swimming In Nature
- Night Sky
- Listening to People Talk About Their Passions
- The Smell Of Old Books, Lilacs, Clean Laundry

12:12am- Imperfect storm

I am starlight in the great proverbial unknowing
The ghastliest predicament

Forgiveness exhaled a tame room
No place for a wilderness
Let alone its wolves

The perfect catalyst for self-realization
Trees, photons and the immeasurably vastness of the night sky
Reminding only of mobility dances through cornerstone comet

Face of me dear moon we meet at last
Am I the glimmer of your eye
Does Hubble speak kindly of us in the Tabloids

Dear songbird midnight moon I am sick
And your brightness my cure
(Don't forget me)
I am dancing inside violent starlights pleasure fits
I am a dead star
Come morning

Inverted Staircase

Watching 8-Bit shadows dance in the dark
Lightning shadow memories shadow songs sing self recognition's to
happier days ahead
I sat out in the rain today
Bring me new gladness
Bring me next chapter air
Bring me soft answers bring me resolutions warm breath bring me
anything but
Ghosts in the stairwell I swallowed
So many shadows I became nothing but

Light

Halftime Piano discord -D ec 4th 2018

Is this all we are
Our current known exchange
Beaming glisten and wild utterance
of another time

Remembered
And made safe
The recognizable defeat
Held together by curious tendons
and apathy
All surmounting it's one archaic
goal

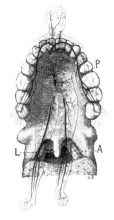

We are dying
We are finding light
In hidden shadows
And reaching once again
Things we thought we buried
A familiar rhetoric between rivals
I silent gazing annihilation of the soul

A coming to earth
She keyed beneath stone decay and inner turmoil
We grow

July 26th 9:21PM, Obi-Wan

You know for a while I would call you "OBI-WAN" in my head. Always my first choice and last hope at goodness in the world. Like the epitome of love incarnate… Even long before I understood why. The feeling of safety available, the ability to be seen, understood and still cared for. To be known and loved for all that you are, feels like

H o m e.

Tuesday July 27th 10:08PM

- Watching planes fly overhead & energetically saying hello to all passengers
- The rhythm of screaming cicada chatter
- Climbing trees
- Finding shiny rocks in the river
- Traveling in a car with people I love
- Constellations on a clear night
- Friends that say I miss you
- Learning a new language
- Eating crepes in a warm diner full of smiles overlooking the pier

Door, Open?

I like to think of it like walking in a
desert following a mirage
The image of it always seems to evade
Draw further away the "Nearer" one
gets

But that is not to say keep walking long
enough there is a large drop off a cliff

And the most beautiful oasis garden
waits for you there
But is that any more real than the
original hallucination itself

Only one way to find out

The streetlamps turn on @ 9:27PM in Indianapolis

Death and poetry and Love and romance of the higher self
These are among the themes in which one may cling to
Should you ever forget what you need

Arms of divine embrace welcome you home through these doors
Though this house is not one to be bought or sold
It is found in the unconditional love available at any moment
There is a light there you see

Made of cedar and jasmine
Welcomes all new eyes new ears for the hearing of
Flame crackles singing sonnet under moonlit reflective pond retina
This is the space we all remember

Cosmic womb
The space from which we came & will return
There is no better time to follow our heart
To break free
To knock on castle door
What awaits on the other side?

Complete freedom
All you have to do is allow
Love in
And love becomes all that is

Wednesday July 28th 10:53PM

- The many variant hues that leaves become in the fall
- Taking nighttime summer walks under streetlamps
- A perfectly ripe avocado
- Hearing a song you haven't heard in quite some time but it

invokes a happy nostalgia

- When friends make you a gift
- The bio-luminescence of Angler fish (Ohh shiny)
- Learning a new musical instrument

Walking barefoot on earth (As opposed to?)

Moths Laugh As Holes

All of my selves are merging and collapsing merging and collapsing

I am a ghost of Purgatory
Afraid of too much light
I am a phantom of shadow memory
I am the paradoxical extreme
I do not know how to exist mildly

Even the moments of peace
Inside the calmest silences
Full of immeasurable vastness

Each multitude
Each epiphany
Each inhale, wave hello
Wave of ocean
Reaching to the sure

Walks by the eyes of street-side stranger

And wonders
Pin me to nearest wall like string-lights so that I keep away your darkness
And that I
Might finally face my fears

Your grandmothers painting

The earth of me rotates in counter-intuitive actions
Until made light from within inner working of clockwork subconscious
Is there not always new chamber
Waiting to be a bright room
Is there not always a larger frame
waiting to admire
Both up close and from a distance

Curtains drawn reverence within multi-dimensional acceptance

Is this love? These mountains we climb?
Artwork of the heart
The certitude of bird-winged hope coo's softly at sunrise
Chirps; "remember me?"

How could I forget -The us of ancient exaltation

We sing, we sing, we sing

Not as sole minded beings
But of ever encapsulating heart space
Breaths warm coastal promise
Newly known
kept safe

The water holds our knowing
Just as the earth may hold us

Friday Night July 30th

- Prisms/Light refraction
- Worn-in clothing that makes you feel safe
- The momentary high of getting a new tattoo and you feel more yourself
- Bravery of flowers perfume smelling strongest right before they die
- The clarity after a big crie
- Vintage lacy dresses
- The way in which smoke caries itself through various airflow
- Superposition
- eye contact
- awkward Segways in conversations that weren't meant to be

8ut4u

Gonna climb a tree to Jupiter

Gonna set fire to the moon

I've always been a travell'n spirit

But my tracks are stopp'n soon

because I've Been so many places
I have seen so many things

Well I looked beneath each rock and cove for a meaning I 'd believe

you see I found exactly what I thought id never dream to be
That all the while
After all those years
What I sought out was right there
in front of me

Sprinklers Come on @ 2:16AM

Love makes us do things we don't understand

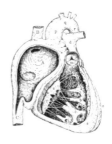

Friday July 30th 11:32PM

- The Impossible brightness of lightning inside storm clouds
- oat milk
- Friends who send you songs or play music for you
- Warm smell of pines in summer wind
- Maharishi Effect
- Echo of frogs across pond water
- the energy of community that accompanies camping with friends
- Telepathy
- Exploring with no destination

Wednesday July 14th 8:52PM, A Cool Cave

The cicadas scream at dusk
It sounds like a warning
Sounds like an invitation sounds like opportunistic fortunes I am once
again not who I was

I am tapping into God-mode the only way I know how
I have just deleted social media
I am staring into the sun
I am taking the leap I am healing the trauma I am facing my fears I am
opening new doors I am still afraid and that's okay
I am loved I am loved I am loved I am loved I am loved I am loved I am
loved I am loved I am loved I am love I am love I am love I am light I am
light I am light I am god
God is love God is love God is love
I deserve love I deserve love I deserve love I deserve happiness I deserve
happiness I deserve safety I deserve abundance nice things
I deserve an easy fun adventurous life with equally reciprocated love &
wealth of the heart mind soul)

-Angels live in my peripheral vision-

Chapter 2- Mirror Room

Dizzy Rainy Guitar Day-Tuesday Aug 10th

The truth

Sometimes I still have trouble letting people in. I close myself off from those who love me and only want to help. I am learning to *Trust*. To be gentle, to be kind. I do not want to be a brute.
I am kind, and I want to live in soft surrender to divine flow of life.

I have gone so long in this haze.
I feel it lifting now, even as I write

We're all a beautiful mess of entropic wonder, self-imploding time bombs only to come back stronger each time.

Mantra

I will focus on the good
I will let people love me
I will believe their compliments
I will love myself
I do love myself
I feel home

I will never stop perceiving new heights

Ohman

Airports and airports and airports and airports and wheels leading
themselves nowhere and the dogs that guide the blind
An announcement on an intercom
A fearful memory that isn't mine
Where the fuck are we all going

I want to answer that in a clever way that has already been done before but
that's already been done before so I will answer it so
And I talk about the going
And nothing new
But maybe in a special order

The a r r I v a l
Of secondary realization

We are in love
With the perpetual being

Alive

Thursday Sep 2nd 10:30AM- Do not blame the serpent

Poems had always hurt
The way life had always hurt
I buried myself in the garden of Eden
Spoke every broken tongued language grasp as half disclosed sanity,
trembling,
discarded
Divided halfhearted vibrant attempts HOPE AT NEW LOVE
I found lovers eyes at sunrise
That day your voice met mine
You saved my life
Through telephone line
In the sky

I CRASH landed
Laughing at how beautiful a broken rib can be
I am not broken anymore
I am the garden
I am the birdsong, singing gentle reminder
whispers
"Darling"

If nothing else at least you know how to fly
How to die and how to live
And on the 3rd day

Live like your life depends on it

Darling you are the moonlight through trees
Broken lover balcony singing sonnet
How much time has passed
I worry
Too
Often
And not enough
About you
And your light
And everyone beneath it

I worry not often enough as the trees
As the moon hold light and all the while
Lets it go
Each night as if a
Prayer
For the wicked
The light-less
Streetways
That which I live
I pray for you everyday

It's never been enough

THE MAGICIAN

In friends we trust

During certain times in my life I am either incredibly close to those I
call my friends
Or I have this pitting hole of soft empty
L I n g e r I n g
Haunting of how things are
Different now
And then again
It goes on like that

These words a time capsule
Hand written love across the centuries carefully stowed away in journal
tomb pages amidst the withering flower petal, fortune cookie wish, tea bag
handle sayings, receipts, candy wrapper concert ticket leaf glitter old stamp
POLAROID prayers

Don't you see? It's us

We're the poetry

13.)

I have found in times of great
Darkness

: (:

Is best to bring balance
By means of extreme positive
Action

14.)

Spell speak
The Past undone
A break tomorrow
A new path comes

15.)

I have kissed deaths soft mouth and said
"Use me anytime"
I like the way misery tastes

Justification Of The Elements

Praise be to the eternal sky eyes

A gathering of holy spring

Tears & open mouth sobs

Arithmetic heartbeat not to be measured only observed

Obscure as heaven herself

As hands become earth

For the holding for the holding

Exhale me no longer

Only feathers fall here

The world itself is a heavy thing
You too
Are here to remember how to be

Weightless

Rising Rising

I sing the song of heavens choir

A candle lit from funeral pyre

The future past burns bright it seems

But heavy hearts grow common themes

The light of truth in new dawn gleams

Telescope eyes

Another veil of reality has lifted

There is are waves of awakening

We are bridging a timeline between heaven and earth

Seeing glimpses of our highest potential, we are inspired in new ways

Breaking out of toxic connections that served it's higher purpose and are forging new connections now

Inside this timeline many of us discovered our "Wings"

To transcend the Kali-Yuga we had to face our darkness so that we could transmute it

The inner world reflects the outer
And in very moment we choose what we wish to experience

As you continue to rise and expand in awareness you will begin to perceive the infinite possibility of your own human nature

The version of you living your dream life, already exists within yourself

How does this version of you

THINK?

FEEL?

ACT?

Does This Count as A Title?

I will admit before I go
The thick of it is to simply let yourself succeed

We are all destined for greatness
But we hold ourselves back

I urge you
To surrender to the pull that alleviates your own suffering
Do not pray to pain but instead welcome experience as it comes
Talk often to your wounds
But not from them
Accept yourself
To the best of your ability
As a being that is completely whole
Butdo not lose sight of the paradoxical human nature
Of a "Better" wholeness
It is why we are here now
To give
To learn
And to love

That is all it takes
To succeed

If not now, when?

You must think I'm a fool
I believe in running headfirst into anything that frightens me

I believe there is immense breakthrough
Directly on the other side of fear
One day I may let it kill me
Should I wander too far up
Cliffs edge of tiptoe
On top of ever lessening shallow pool

Dancing looks a lot like drowning
To be fully immersed
A sort of zolted surrender

Oh god what you must think of me
That's it
Maybe you are my biggest
fear

Quantum entanglement

Sometimes I am

E
V
E
R
Y
W
H
E
R
E

At once

Other times

I am

Hello desert moon

Nice of you to idle by I twist and turn, I swell in June, I left you tracks I'm drifting soon

The sky trees reflect kind mind likeness down upon you

Sharing light that doesn't burn

Do you hear it now too?

The harmonics of earth turns and

face of revelation that which is

perpetually said

But remains unspoken

We died the first time, 11 years ago

Is my hair still black raven song

Am I the moonlight

Can you hear me?

20.)

Tonight I am thinking of the ocean
And what it means to kill

And I think of the human predicament
Of breathing
And the arms that are water
And I think in comparison

The demonization of sharks (Why)
And both oceanic ability to take a life

If somebody drowns
No one curses the ocean
At least not enough to broadcast
But shark eaten
And sharks become murderous

Does difference in blame lay in situated consciousness
And/or the ability to look at the self

Or do things just

H a p p e n

God winks in synchronicity, angels laugh in patience

When it's bad

I am to go to sleep soon
So as to not worsen
But I feel with great urgency the importance that I try and explain what it's
like maybe for anyone who needs it--

I come back as consciousness
That burns through my eyes replicated out onto paper
But my memory is shot
I exist then only every 3rd sentence or so
The size of rooms change
Entire perception of spatial comprehension is shattered
And I worry here
Mostly about the pressure in my head
Like being underwater too long
Which way is up
My bod feels incredibly far away with attention as quick and numb as ever

I feel very vulnerable
Every faint noise is a potential threat

Half of the words in my head are neglected conversation;
A stupid song that I love
Something about nails on chalkboard
But it doesn't stop
None of the conversation is good
Either neutral or awful
Falling asleep

Again
To move feels impossible

Was I always this bad
Has anyone ever actually seen who I am

Who AM I
And why
And why

Probably… Love

The End

Starlight Happening

It is important to understand
That not everything we think to be true

That what you believe about your own being
Is not inherently factual and may be the effect of any plethora of hidden
cognitive programming's whether it be childhood teachings or television
subliminals
There is an inherent hive mentality throughout the human collective that
operates separate from Source
Anything outside of source is false and must be worked with carefully
through self healing, analysis, re-parenting and so on. Most importantly
Understand everyone around you operates from a different mode of being.
These modes then create our separate and individually perceived realities

Alchemists Playground

Hazy courtyard dark
Eyelid bedroom sonnet sunrise
And happy endless windows lets call them next door neighbors

A courtesy

Always asking the right questions
Don't look down don't look in eyes too long hello next to nothing
manuscript we call ourselves civilized and I think my plants are my
favorite people
I am becoming a good process
Which is to say I am already the unafraid

A frequency

Those of you walking through hell

You are the bridge to heaven

S elf-Help poetry

Stop saying you can't do
something

There is an immensely vast
universe that hatched you into being
It is up to you to fulfill your
highest narrative

Kill the voice that says you
can't
The part of you waiting to be
borne is on the other side of the wall

You have waited lifetimes to
break down

Chapter 3-
Sanctuary

Atmospheric Algebra

I am seeing rainbow prism
Etched into the atmosphere
Like they belong

I cannot explain what it means because I do not know the depth of your
understanding
I can only attempt to explain my own relative perception
Of light, of refraction, of human purpose mostly above all

I am present
I am seeing
I am seeking
I am becoming

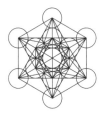

I exist

Thursday Jan 16th

We will call ourselves magicians
From the things that we have seen
Dancing moonlight whiskey phantoms
You will have thought it was a dream

And a dream I am no longer
I am a moniker of things
And we know quite well how to vanish
When day in's lose their gleam
I'm a fanciful machine
Keeping time in my mental mind
Becomes less rigid while upstream

But I still can't swim, and I live off whim

At least now I know what it means

A brand new set of eyes

Living inside of nightfall now
With the day adorned in
Heavens light
Each new breath be step towards Grace towards
The resurrection
Of hope

Clarity magnified in unity of the heavens gate to give thanks for each
path each encounter
Opens the heart to new experience and the shadows will not conquer

A hope here
Within the echo of familiar sunlight warm as embrace I hope we find
strength
To fight
To choose to rise up

When destiny presents uncertainty
I will meet you there

At the edge of the earth

Wing-ed and new
Ready to jump

(-Sky Dive Oregon!
Don't hold back, take the leap. -Bus Divination)

Sympathetic Resonance

If you ever find yourself off kilter of happiness I am here to remind
you
That your own heaven exists

But it is entirely up to you to find it

Stop getting in your own way

You are love incarnate

Always have a north star pulling you forward

You have suffered so much

In your earthly body

That you have come to associate suffering with love

This is simply not true

Love is divine and pure

Sees you as its own

Reflection

You are whole

Just as you are

A word about the noise

Humanity is going through one of the biggest evolution of
consciousness ever experienced
We are collectively being asked to re-evaluate everything we thought we
knew so as to bring about necessary intuitive knowing, secondary to our
"Factual" 3D modes of being

We are rising into our own divinity of conscious understanding
This will help harbor in the resonance of new earth which is to be based in
unity rather than separation

Remember to keep love in your hearts and do not lose focus due to the
shadow of this earth
Things are being brought to light now so that darker aspect of the human
function may be eradicated
The timing of everything in the world is of no coincidence

Perfume Of The Gods

They   say   fear   dies   like   flowers
Becoming   increasingly   loud-scented
Moments   before   death

And   what   then   becomes   us
But bravery

Have you seen my wallet?

There is nothing more enticing than the breath of cool lungs over hot
pavement irreplaceable as glass balcony scenery of mind windows
landscape
Are we dancing or are we millionaires come morning?
All I know is the low hum of heater vent reminds me of the future
summer I will meet the love of my life
He wears soft hooded garment on warm pavements
Breathes coolness down my spine like this run-on sentence mouth of
mine
The moment that eyes become doorways become question

When it happens, I will let you know

Exposition of opposites

It is said that to understand others
you must first understand your
deepest self
The person in the mirror will only
reflect that which is of relative
truth
What you believe you become

And it is for this reason
I urge you to be nobody

At all

Syncopated cyanide

The dizzy rhythms of dancy heartbeat streets under moonshape tree
canopy
A familiar yet fixated transpose
Messy entanglement the atoms, bright like refurbished furniture if only
for the housing
I have seen this many times before you know
The madness behind melody

When all that's left to do
Is dance

We're In For It Now

Have you ever noticed if you slow your breathing, it's said to slow the
momentum in the hands of a clock
I don't know much about gravity

Or good posture
But I believe in good things
I believe in the importance of a simple hello
I believe that we are all incredibly intricate constellations dressed up in
business suit and scarlet
Just waiting for the right moment

Waiting for the right

Waiting for

waiting

The Dissection Of Opposite Equilibrium

Happening suddenly and nowhere at once
I felt my heart palpitations become cosmic benevolence through the
light of the eyes of some near sky heaven
Lit up like Reno Neva crosswalks
Lit up like Jupiter
Lit up like Sunday sunrise the weekend you had brunch with your
mother at the local dimlit diner
The small fiery synapse each spark a new miracle in you

To finally
Wake up happy

The Silver Linings Pot Of Gold Was A Storm

There are things in this world worth mentioning
And there are things that play beyond the ordinary perception of
hearing
Human bodies shift as the seasons glean obstinate to their own crude
warmth
The heat of first bloom
Eternal spring you were a windy season
And I, your desert daydream

To love anything is to give eternal life

Silverware rhetoric

The silverware has laden themes
As china cabinets finer things
And here the glass has threads and strings
It does not break
It threads our dreams

Nudes At Band Practice

Am I heaven-sent am I hellbound in my nightmares I hear hellhounds
I lived underground in the sediments
Now I'm sentimental partially insane
Become a desert you'll pray for rain and start to bloom despite your
pain

So good thing there's no tomorrow
Living life like a penny borrowed
Like a dime-piece inside your thoughts when life never goes like you
thought it ought

Sometimes it's even better

Friends and laughter, handholds through sweaters
Early sunrise watching birds together

So, keep your head up, despite the weather

Dissection of Brain Soup

Maybe we are not starfish
But I like the way the body heals

Maybe we are not music
But there is no greater sound than a friendly "Hello" from a loved one

Maybe we are no longer dead stars, contemplating our own innermost
vastness
But my how I have seen the whole universe in the breathe of a single
moment

In the way your eyes heal me
In the music that is your voice

In the impossible brightness of your human smile

I think I like you

Perennial Valentine

Over the last few years my soul grew very restless

Peeling skin-bark off the bones of trees that do not change
How do they adapt through each condition
And yet to naked eye; remain unchanged

Some people too are evergreen
Some people are chameleon leaving exoskeleton shedding across every
continent

Survival was never guaranteed
And I have seen now enough broken branches to light a fire higher
than Jupiter

I have seen the inner wardrobe reflection of our appearance go
unnoticed for centuries leaving warm spots on cool rocks
I have been both and I have been the neither than notices

I think the point then
Is to simply
Do what makes you happy

Broken Schematics

There are multitudes of ways to say goodbye
Many of which may go unnoticed
Throughout the cinema of our internal grounds keeping
The watchers of ascent as halo wings sprout from every earthly action

I get it

You said there are only two things that make a man memorable
The amount that he sticks to his word
And the last words that he sticks to

Doomsday Ambigram

I think that night we broke through
I think heaven opens mouth wide the way death opens funeral gate I
think we won something
I think it all gets better from here

There is soft thunder laugh flashing dancing killing of orchids
resurrected in moonlit sonata let me be Frank

It was 2/22/2022
The sky cracked open music sprang from every orifice of cloud pore
The love comes in waves

We are the new generations
And we are tired of waiting
Through the belly of beasts we landed on soft moss of earth shoe-less
and hungry
Fed by love itself
The old Gods feast through us
Move through our very tongues

And we speak only truth

Remind me again, your favorite song?

Divine Intervention

Have you ever experienced
A run on sentence
That felt like your whole life was a wrong turn
Blood coughing mouth smile neon signs light up skyward

"This is the way!" And they will be right
Until you stop listening to the radio long enough stop staying asleep in
stranger's backseat vomiting address like 1950's talk show host
Driver says --where to next honey"

Must be a bad dream a bad drug blaming all external nauseations on
the new altruistic demigods
As clean won as Superbowl lottery junkies screaming maddened at the
moon for not having been borne rich
I know what you're thinking

And
You're probably right
It's up to you

The Day The Orchids Fell

Do you think the sky smiles as rain?
Or is it sadness, the likened pools

Does despair hold the same frequency in post-modern Japan?
As a US congressman cheats on his wife
there's news in the papers but the truth is far more devastating

We are fed distractions like cheap wines expense hath no taste to the
illiterate
But my darling where does your soul reside once the bars close once
the telemarketer hangs up
What do you feed your anger?

Eyes of Babylon the earth is hungry for new devastation's
There is promise in your fingertips

In your crooked laughter
I hear the underlying hope

And it to, dances
It too, sings
It too, cries wishing for a resurrection

All the while
It will not die

Yet eternally transformed

Oh Toronto

Paint splatter rhythmic solitude whispers quiet transgressions barks
hope rabid sanity throughout moonscaped city lantern dancy raintop old
houses

Dreaming never felt so safe
Like walking off a cliff forgetting you are the gravity

To fall
And be caught

Transcendental Dish Soap

A myriad of dancing shapes float before my eye
I think I think too many thoughts about the pillars nye
And if I give a weary groan to places far and near
Please know that I'm of rightful mind
My sanity is clear

-Letter from kitchen sink

You Tell Me

How much else have we forgotten
Starved us clean our souls begotten
Fruit then falls more time for
wrought-Ing

And just when u think you know who you ought to be
The new soft earth will help you clearly see
That seasons come &Seasons grow, and human plants reap what we
sow

We sew each other back together
Like argyle patterns in ugly sweater

But no man on earth is truly doomed
We bump around in dark lit rooms
Hallucinating Jesus Mary mother's womb

Until the night gives way to day
Our sorrows then will wash away

What else have we forgotten
But that our hearts were meant for talking
That our leaves were built to bloom

And dammit man
Not a day too soon

Wedding Bells In The Bookstore

I know for certain there are quiet moments between pause breathe
where your eyes still train new mind new thought forms subjective
sentence oceanic pooling's inside the cave hearts of men flipping pages,
betting wages that life and death will always phase us
Plateau thinking is contagious

Just listen to the rhythm of your ancestor dance through each cell in
your body their memories trance
And if for now your soul advance

Then Lila be the name

Supernova Likes Long Walks

Who am I?
Who am I?
The Ego asked the moon

I think I've been away too long
I'll be returning soon

I've crossed every treacherous SEE
Crossed every endless shore
And no matter where we travel to
The Ego asks for more

The heart chimes in so gentle
As soft as quiet rain
Says "Kid I see you've traveled far,
Through loneliness and pain."

The heart spoke of the sun
Said don't you worry now

That all your roads bring beautiful things
Green pastures, linens, cows
For these places you have traveled
May have been gruesome in their day
But every broken beaten path
Was walked to pave the way
By each new road that's made
You leave a trail behind
This path you walked, now lights the way
For other hearts to find

The moon in her soft orbit
The sun plays tag in time

"Who am I"
Asked the universe

The day the stars aligned

Castle In The Sky Rent Free

Dance across my halo
I don't have a care so

Take me as I am take me as I am
Messy bits of rhetoric
Things spun inside dreams

Are we having fun yet? Is it as crazy as it seems?

I know it all feels sudden
I know your heart feels sad
To share the depth of potency
In time will make us glad
The strangers walk the street-side
The stars all sing in tune
We are a part of bigger things
I know you'll hear it soon
We are a cosmic rhythm
We are a mark of fame
If anything comes of our lives
Don't dare to make it tamed

We are the earth soft spirit
We are the gladness there
We are the water, wind and sky

You never know who you might be
If you don't care to try

Mahasamadhi

There is so much stuff at any given moment
That of which after any extent of analysis I can always
Reduce to it's utmost simplicity

And there is nothing more to say than

I love you,

Thank you for never giving up.

The roof
"Be in the world, but not of it."

Everything I could ever want is right here
Everything that has sparked inspiration or nostalgia is right here
Everything anybody could ever want
Is always within reach
Fireflies
airplanes
Bats flying across streetlamps
Warm fire from the neighbors yard
A good book
People who love you in close vicinity
Cicada
The comfort of trees
Wind
An acoustic guitar
The moon and starlight
A smile
Hope in my heart
I am so thankful to everyone who has ever supported my weirdness

Here's to a summer spent on a rooftop

May you always find comfort wherever you are

-Cat

Manufactured by Amazon.ca
Bolton, ON

32973180R00048